For Mom, who taught me to love Yo-Yo Ma and the Bach cello
suites by blasting them too early on Saturday mornings.
You are my bridge across so many borders. —J.H.

To Santiago Martínez —T.M.

Playing at the Border: A Story of Yo-Yo Ma
Text copyright © 2021 by Joanna Ho
Illustrations copyright © 2021 by Teresa Martinez
All rights reserved. Manufactured in Italy.
No part of this book may be used or reproduced in any manner whatsoever without written permission except in the case
of brief quotations embodied in critical articles and reviews. For information address HarperCollins Children's Books, a
division of HarperCollins Publishers, 195 Broadway, New York, NY 10007.

www.harpercollinschildrens.com

Library of Congress Control Number: 2020946935
ISBN 978-0-06-299454-7

The artist used Adobe Photoshop to create the digital illustrations for this book.
Typography by Chelsea C. Donaldson
21 22 23 24 25 RTLO 10 9 8 7 6 5 4 3 2 1

First Edition

Playing at the Border

A Story of Yo-Yo Ma

By Joanna Ho

Illustrated by Teresa Martinez

HARPER

An Imprint of HarperCollinsPublishers

On the banks of the Rio Grande,

feet planted on the soil of one nation,
eyes gazing at the shores of another,
Yo-Yo Ma played a solo
accompanied by an orchestra of wind and water.

Fed by the snowcapped mountains of Colorado
and flowing into the Gulf of Mexico,
the Rio Grande became a boundary
dividing two countries
that used to be one.

Yo-Yo Ma made music
on riverbanks that separated people into
Mexican
American
citizen
immigrant.

Though
They,
     We,
were,
        are
one.

Feet planted on the soil of one nation,
facing the shores of another,

Yo-Yo Ma closed his eyes
as music poured from his heart
through his hands.

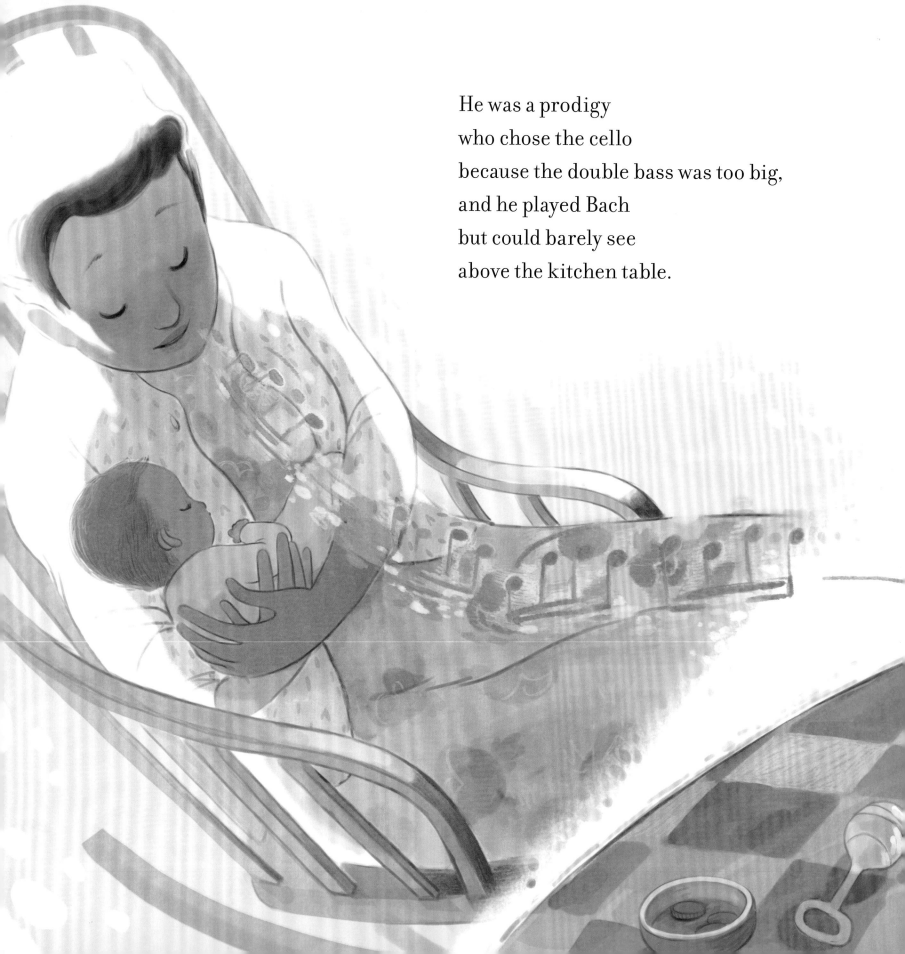

He was a prodigy
who chose the cello
because the double bass was too big,
and he played Bach
but could barely see
above the kitchen table.

Precise placement of his fingertips
produced perfect notes
memorized when he was four—
three years before he performed
for Presidents Eisenhower and Kennedy,
twenty-six years before he won his first Grammy,

forty-seven years before he became
a United Nations Messenger of Peace,
and fifty-two years before he accepted
the Presidential Medal of Freedom.

Born in France
to Chinese parents
and raised in the United States,
Yo-Yo Ma challenges convention
and weaves worlds together.
He designed a garden set to song,

united musicians
across the Silk Road,

and translated classical sounds
into hip-hop movements.

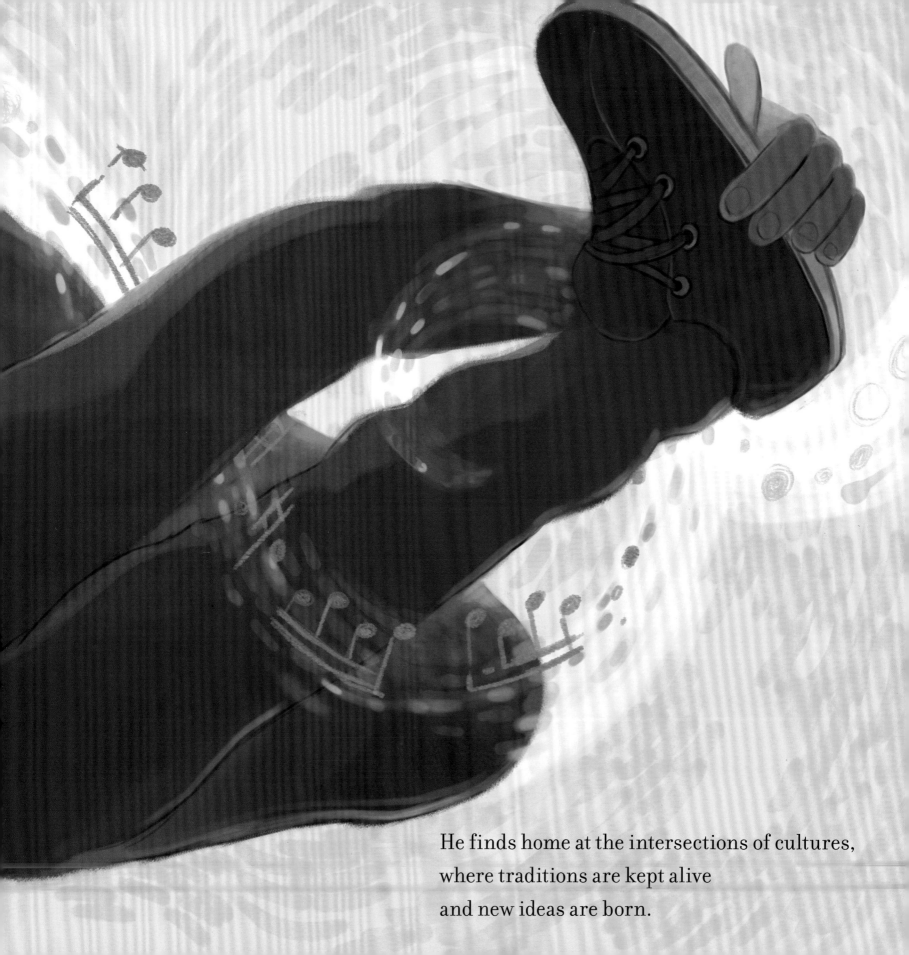

He finds home at the intersections of cultures,
where traditions are kept alive
and new ideas are born.

Feet planted on the soil of one nation,
eyes gazing at the shores of another,

Yo-Yo Ma guided his bow gracefully
back and forth
across the strings of his cello.

Built in Italy,
his cello was made from parts
that came from lands of
many languages.

The stick of the bow
from a tree grown only in Brazil,
the hair of the bow
from a horse's tail in Mongolia,
the ebony frog from a forest in West Africa.
The cello wood's reddish hues dyed
with dragon's blood from Indonesia
and its yellow accents created
with curry powder from India.

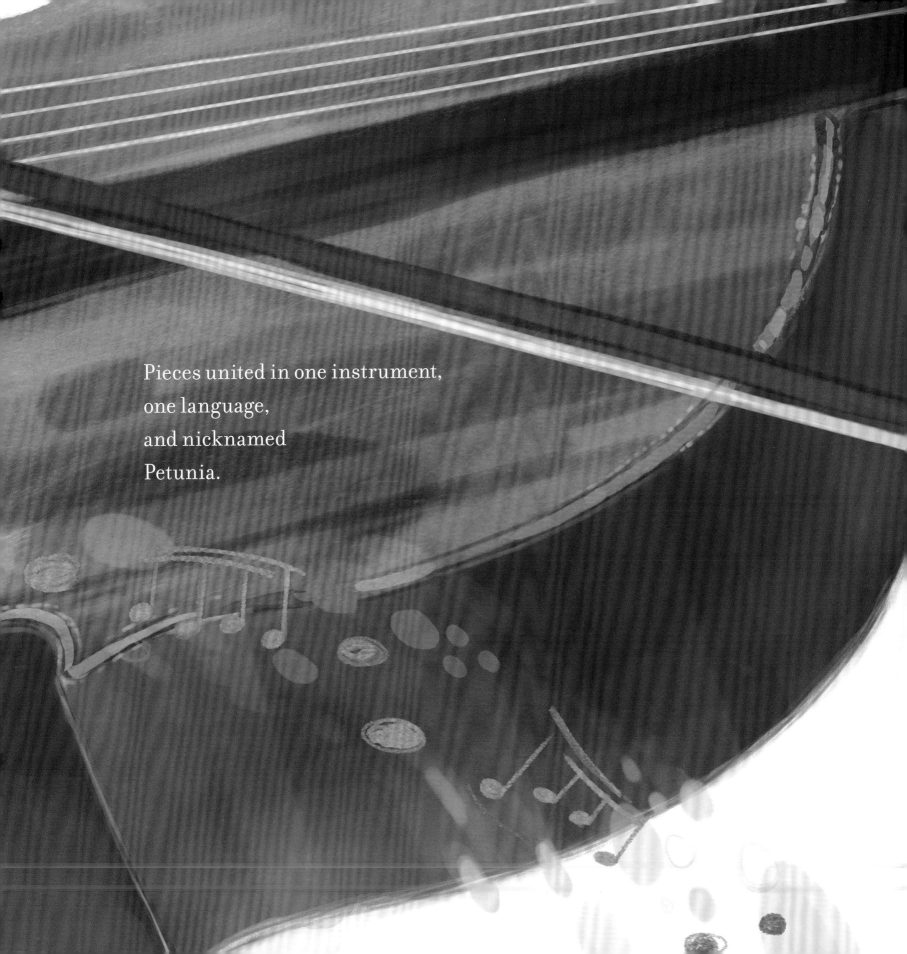

Pieces united in one instrument,
one language,
and nicknamed
Petunia.

Feet planted on the soil of one nation,
eyes gazing at the shores of another,
Yo-Yo Ma coaxed Petunia's strings to sing
Bach's cello suites.
Their notes danced over rocks and rivers
and walls
into the sky.

Composed in Germany
three hundred years before it swooped and soared,
whirled and twirled over the Rio Grande,
this music was nearly forgotten.
It was rediscovered
in a secondhand store in Spain,
then recorded,
revived
more than two centuries after it was written.

Its notes reached
through time,

alive.

Fingers flying over four strings,
Yo-Yo Ma made improbable melodies,
a harmony of notes,
a symphony of sound,
from a single cello.

He played at the border
between nations,
between cultures,

between languages,
between centuries,

and built a bridge.

Yo-Yo Ma: Artist and Creator of Change

Born into a musical Chinese family living in Paris, Yo-Yo Ma was a child prodigy who played and memorized Bach's cello suites when he was only four years old. Yo-Yo's family moved to the United States when he was seven, the same year he performed with his sister—also a musical prodigy—for President John F. Kennedy and former president Dwight D. Eisenhower.

Yo-Yo Ma uses art to push boundaries. Through over one hundred albums—including nineteen Grammy Award winners—he has played classical music, bluegrass, traditional Chinese melodies, Argentine tangos, movie soundtracks, and jazz. In 2000, he brought together musicians from along the Silk Road—a group of strangers who spoke different languages, played different instruments, and came from different cultures—to meet for a workshop. This group grew into the Silk Road Ensemble and shows the world that art transcends political divisions. It has won two Grammy Awards along the way.

Yo-Yo Ma has also collaborated with artists beyond the musical world. In 1999, he worked with landscape architect Julie Moir Messervy to design the Toronto Music Garden, an interpretation in nature of Bach's first cello suite. In 2013, Yo-Yo Ma teamed up with dancer Charles "Lil Buck" Riley to perform "The Swan" by Camille Saint-Saëns, through a style of street dance known as jookin.

A United Nations Messenger of Peace and winner of the Presidential Medal of Freedom, Yo-Yo Ma is more than a musician. He is a leader of positive change in the world.

The Bach Project

In August 2018, Yo-Yo Ma began the Bach Project, a two-year effort to increase global connections through music. On this journey, he performed Johann Sebastian Bach's six suites for solo cello in thirty-six places around the world. Along with his concerts, Yo-Yo Ma

collaborated with local community leaders at each site to plan a day of action to build a more connected future.

Yo-Yo performed at Trinity University in San Antonio, Texas, on April 12, 2019. This was followed by a day of action on the border between the United States and Mexico on April 13. Playing at the border was a powerful symbolic response to the anti-immigrant rhetoric and policies pushed by the president of the United States and his supporters during this time. Joined by leadership and community members from Laredo, Texas, and its sister city across the border, Nuevo Laredo, Mexico, Yo-Yo played an excerpt from Bach's cello suites before addressing the crowd. He said, "As you all know, as you did and do and will do, in culture, we build bridges, not walls."

Why Bach's Cello Suites?

Johann Sebastian Bach (1685–1750), a German musician, is considered one of the greatest composers of all time. When Bach composed the six suites for solo cello, it was considered an accompanying instrument; very few solos were written for the instrument. The original music for Bach's cello suites was lost, and they were all but forgotten for two hundred years.

Thirteen-year-old Catalan cellist Pablo Casals began studying the suites after he found a copy of the music in a thrift shop in Barcelona, Spain. He did not record the music until 1936, when he was sixty years old. Since then, they have become some of the most frequently performed and well-known compositions written for the cello.

These suites are special because they create the sound of harmonizing melodies on one instrument. It is music that seems impossible but is made possible on a single cello. Played on the banks of the Rio Grande, the cello suites united people on both sides of the border in a show of harmony and hope.

Getting to Know Petunia

Yo-Yo Ma's cello was created by Domenico Montagnana in Venice, Italy, in 1733. Nicknamed Petunia by one of Yo-Yo Ma's students, she is worth $2.5 million.

Petunia is made of parts from all over the world. An Indonesian plant called dragon's blood dyed the wood red, while its yellow color was created by curry powder from India. The bow came from pernambuco, a tree grown only in Brazil. The hair on the bow was plucked from a horse in Mongolia or Canada, where the cold weather makes horsehair thicker. The fingerboard and the frog—the black parts of the cello and bow—were made from ebony, a tree grown in West Africa.

Yo-Yo Ma considers his instrument to be his voice. Petunia comes from all over the world, crossing borders and boundaries to unite people through the universal language of music.

Resources:

Cellist Yo-Yo Ma Plays Bach in Shadow of Border Crossing:
    www.npr.org/2019/04/13/713092703/cellist-yo-yo-ma-plays-bach-in-shadow-of-border-crossing
Yo-Yo Ma and the Cello from around the World: www.youtube.com/watch?v=017wU33Jh-M
The Music of Strangers: Yo-Yo Ma and the Silk Road Ensemble. Directed by Morgan Neville.
    Tremolo Productions, 2016.
Yo-Yo Ma: Inspired by Bach's Cello Suites 1 & 2 : The Music Garden & The Sound of the Carceri at
    https://www.youtube.com/watch?v=RQrQvrqwwRE
Spike Jonze Presents: Lil Buck and Yo-Yo Ma: www.youtube.com/watch?v=C9jghLeYufQ

Author's Note:

My mom used to blast a CD of Yo-Yo Ma playing Bach's cello suites early every Saturday morning. As a teenager, I hated it; I just wanted her to turn it off so I could sleep in. She never turned it off. Now the cello suites remind me of her, a woman whose love and strength and power continue to astound me. My mom immigrated to the United States from Taiwan in her early twenties. She didn't have a college degree but hustled to build a life for my family and to give my brother and me the opportunity to dream.

When Yo-Yo Ma played at the border, it was an action of resistance and celebration, a reminder of the worth of immigrants, the work of immigrants, the belonging of immigrants here and everywhere. It felt like an act for me, for my family, and for anyone who has ever moved away from home in order to build a better life.

Yo-Yo Ma builds bridges.
Let us all build bridges, not walls.